EPISTLES TO EVE

And other poems

poems by

Gracia Grindal

Finishing Line Press
Georgetown, Kentucky

EPISTLES TO EVE

And other poems

Copyright © 2024 by Gracia Grindal
ISBN 979-8-88838-538-8 First Edition
All rights reserved under International and Pan-American Copyright Conventions. No part of this book may be reproduced in any manner whatsoever without written permission from the publisher, except in the case of brief quotations embodied in critical articles and reviews.

ACKNOWLEDGMENTS

Curiosities, Evil, and Death were originally published in *The Christian Century*.
Winter Funeral, Norway originally published in *Simil*
The Country Where We Belong originally published in *The Lutheran Forum*

Publisher: Leah Huete de Maines
Editor: Christen Kincaid
Cover Art: Tom Maakestad
Author Photo: Liv Anda Knatterud
Cover Design: Tom Maakestad

Order online: www.finishinglinepress.com
also available on amazon.com

Author inquiries and mail orders:
Finishing Line Press
PO Box 1626
Georgetown, Kentucky 40324
USA

Contents

EPISTLES TO EVE

I	STARTING OVER	1
II	TOUCH	2
III	SINGING	3
IV	TRUST	4
V	TASTE	5
VI	SPEECH	6
VII	DEATH	7
VIII	CEREMONIES	8
IX	REPAIRING THE RUINS	9
X	RAISING THE MANCHILD	10
XI	FOOD	11
XII	ILLNESS	12
XIII	DYING	13
XIV	EVIL	14
XV	THE FUNERAL	15
XVI	TRUTH	16
XVII	FEAR	17
XVIII	LAW	18
XIX	FORM	19
XX	EARTH	20
XXI	WATER	21
XXII	AIR	22
XXIII	BREAD OF LIFE	23
XXIV	ANOTHER GARDEN	24
XXV	LOVE	25
XXVI	REMEDY	26
XXVII	FAREWELL	27
XXVIII	THE TURN	28
XXIX	ETERNITY	29
XXX	MYSTERY	30
XXXI	CURIOSITIES	31
XXXII	FIRE	32
XXXIII	COURAGE	33

THE GATE OF HEAVEN AND OTHER POEMS

THE GATE OF HEAVEN	37
EPITHALAMION	38
MOVING IN	40

EPIGRAMS

PROLOGUE 43
SOCIAL SECURITY 44
BAPTISM 45
WILD OATS 46
WORTHLESS, HEARTFELT ADVICE 47
A BODY KNOWS 48
NURSERY RHYME 49
GENETIC CODE 50
THE EXCHANGE 51
NEGATIVE RESEARCH 52
WINTER ROSE 53
WINTER FUNERAL, NORWAY 54
CHRISTMAS CAROL 55
THIS LITTLE SONG 56

THE COUNTRY WHERE WE BELONG

I	VISION 59
II	THE WAY 60
III	THE FEAR OF GOD 61
IV	HOLY SCRIPTURE 62
V	HOPE 63
VI	TURNING TOWARD THINGS ETERNAL 64
VII	COUNSEL OF COMPASSION 65
VIII	PURITY OF HEART 66
IX	WISDOM 67
X	THE SHAPE OF ELOQUENCE 68
XI	ELOQUENT WISDOM 69
XII	THE PLENITUDE OF JOY 70

THE ROSE 71

AUTHOR'S BIO 73

EPISTLES TO EVE

(Dedicated to Bryn Anders on his 37th birthday)

I

STARTING OVER

These epistles of our ending I send to you,
Dear Eve. I want your knowledge as tyrants mock
Centuries of careful thought that helped us through.
I crave the curiosities you sought
Built into high temples raised by faith
Now dusty fragments drifting away like sand,
Columns of graceful marbles splintered to death,
Apocalyptic ashes in my hand.
Tell me, now in the darkness evil brings,
How the fiery swords came into play
Forcing you out of Eden with your things
Leaving behind the garden of a perfect day.
You had to study nature to begin
Raising a world of culture from your sin.

II

TOUCH

How did Adam learn to read your face,
The portents in your eyes, the ardor there,
Using his finger to draw your contours and trace
Your feelings, memories that lovers share?
Aping the lines he set into his own lips,
Raising an eyebrow as he tried to feel
How the heart rises in our chests and is gripped
By a mirrored look, how the planets wheel
In your eyes, teaching each other how bodies rhyme,
Growing in knowledge, like a baby learns
To make a face for joy or sorrow, then in time
Naturally weeps as her own passion burns.
Teach us to read, freed of our eyeless masks,
Aspects of features in a dimple's dance.

III

SINGING

Singing comes first, a baby humming along
Before sound breaks like waves into words.
Hearing her mother's music: her body's song
Beats in the cells where its rhythms can be heard;
Marking the measures in her mother's breast,
Catches of melodies she sings alone
While frying eggs after a night of rest.
Choruses of psalms in waking bones
Make concerts in our bodies yearning for choirs
Echoing together in one voice, to sing praise
To one who traced auricles of sound in us, desires
For harmony. Listen! the virus says
Silence, stopping the music. Dear Mother Eve,
Teach us again melodies we can believe.

IV

TRUST

Your company and image like a mirror
Reflected him. You saw and learned to trust
His moods echoing in you. Without fear
Daring to hold him, embrace his mortal dust,
And unafraid, sharing the light of day
Dappling on rays of morning through the leaves.
You practiced freedom, it filled your heart with tunes
Not noted in the scales of law. Now, Eve,
Blue bureaucrats forbid it, we cannot croon
Melodies of liberty. They write
Policies stilling our singing hearts.
I see you ambling through fecund Paradise
Free from a hand that issues in the dark
Decrees banning the company we keep,
Etchings of Eden fading in our sleep.

V

TASTE

The fragrances of Eden made the meal,
Redolent bouquets of summer wine
From nectars in the sweet Elysian fields
Intoxicating brews, tasty, divine.
We fed on delicacies, ambrosian food.
A scene from Paradise: the waiter brings
Dishes from Eve's kitchen, elegant and good.
The presentation fit for a row of kings,
Evenings that linger in gardens of memory
Banned for us now, shuttered by mandates
A King Canute of bitters signs, decrees
Against our gathering at table, to celebrate.
The monarch hides in his mansion, eats his fill,
As the full tide rises, his vintage chills.

VI

SPEECH

Adam named the animals with words
He knew from where? How did you master speech,
How did you fathom the language you first heard
Moving and eloquent? How did he teach
His tongue to you, or did Eden stamp
Its syntax on his rib great nature's code?
Knowledge shone in the groves like a lamp.
Curious, you longed to study, then God strode
Into the garden, canceling your school.
Ruined, and banished to a world of pain
Where hard labor teaches us nature's rules
Not reckoned in proclamations. They are not plain
To the industries that keep us from finding out
Corruption bankrupting words, inflaming doubt.

VII

DEATH

You had to shape your habits by yourself,
How to face death, unknown until his blood
Soaked into earth, shrieking to you like hell,
To raise his body sinking into the mud.
You reached for Adam, holding him for grief
Wiping away your salt tears with his hand.
Hating and loving Cain, the murderer and thief
Of your loves. You hallowed the virgin land
With his remains. Now we crouch in our homes
Without ceremony, fearful of touch.
Like Adam raised up out of the garden loam,
With no relatives, unable to figure much.
He longed for congress in the green outside
Empty as Good Friday absent a son who died.

VIII

CEREMONIES

A ceremony we kept for centuries
Handing down to the young their family lore:
Here's what we eat on Christmas Eve:
Succulent spareribs like the year before,
The meat browned and roasted, potatoes mashed
With gravy, just like grandma always made,
Customs tracking long before we can ask,
That we must practice so the ritual never fades—
Now they are stopped. Simple human rites
Need repetition, you taught Seth new routines
That tempered him, rendered him polite
Against pure instinct, savage, brutal and mean.
You taught him manners training him to be kind,
To hold back for Adam, to train his mind.

IX

REPAIRING THE RUINS

To build an Eden out of brokenness
Now that the angels stand with their fiery swords
Banning your coming back. All you had left
Ran in your dreams of perfect worlds restored,
But never found. You had to shape a place
From fragments, and chopped timbers down to build
A haven, writing the rules keeping you safe,
An armistice banged out against our guilt
Keeping you by the hearth, its roaring fire,
Fearing vandals breaking into your peace.
Now you must face forward against desire,
Building a width of paradise out of beams.
The walls and thick studs keeping the chaos out,
Synecdoches of Eden in your house.

X

RAISING THE MANCHILD

Teach us again how you civilized the child.
You bore him in a stable of blossoms, red
As the passion that made him, animal and wild;
The gestures to rein him in, curbing your dread
He would step off into air and plunge
Into a chasm of hurt you could not heal.
Raging at Adam as you watched him lunge—
Your fears making your mother's senses reel.
Drowning his childhood in the water's spray
Leaping toward manhood, leaving you behind,
Gaining the strength to keep evil at bay,
Keen to match his courage and his mind;
Able to flex his muscles and keep you safe
His father's lineaments in him, courteous, brave.

XI

FOOD

Passing through the garden, you would point:
This red berry is poison, leave it for the birds,
Lore we have almost lost, labels our coin.
Today the arteries of commerce are words
We cannot tell are true. Did you taste
The juice, letting it deaden your tongue or watch
Animals for wisdom? Hunger, fearing the waste,
Plucked them for supper, set them by in a box,
Then threw them out, blood onto the snows,
Sweeping over the fields like crimson death.
Winter shut you inside, the waters froze,
Blizzards making visible your breath
Your shelves deep with the sustenance you stored
To keep famine's horse from trampling open your door.

XII

ILLNESS

They issue edicts against invisible germs
Whose parliaments gather in learned cells.
Unschooled in abstract legal terms
They do battle, making our old bones swell
With weapons of their war. When Adam caught a cold
Chilled by the dank miasmas from the ground,
How did you treat it? Give him a physic, and fold
His infection in wool from the sheep you found,
Learning to card and spin to keep him warm?
You waited the body's fine defenses to heal
The ague, doctoring him with your human arms,
You had no measures or edicts to make him feel
Better. Only nature's medics did him good
As fever heated and healed his sanguine blood.

XIII

DYING

We have put by the rituals of death.
Banned from the bedside of our relatives
As they brave the darkness, gasping their final breaths
Not holding them, flesh to flesh, with no reprieve
Keeping the contract with our nearest kin
To care for them, we peer through walls of glass,
Press against windows, panes chilling our skin.
Fearing mortality, we watch them pass
Without a tune, a scent, or touch that binds
Their bodies to us. You shaped the ritual
Of touch, hand to hand, that stirs our kind,
Parchment skins of words longing to tell
The young weeping outside them how to live
Rich with testaments they are dying to give.

XIV

EVIL

When you thrust your hand into the green leaves
For knowledge, to see, to taste, to be divine,
You trusted his promise, his hissing lies, dear Eve,
The great deceiver bidding you to dine,
To bite into fragrant, forbidden food.
As you armed yourself for sin, a luscious meal,
He called good evil and pure evil good.
Did the serpent snapping at your heels
Laugh when the fruit began crawling with worms?
Sin's dark shadows deepen, we behold,
Surging around us in a crown of germs,
Illusions writhing inside the apple's gold.
Demons swarming out of a broken trust,
Beggared of goods, wanton with Eden's dust.

XV

THE FUNERAL

Where did you garner words for the last good-bye,
Putting Abel back into the dust
From which he came, after he had died.
Rigor mortis, foul with rank odors of must;
Calling the relatives to help you grieve,
Finding the women who could make the lunch,
Buttering the sandwiches while you, bereaved,
August and regal, let your tears be staunched
By courtesies of mourning: the prayers, the speech,
Suited up with sorrow, familiar words
Now faces droning over lines that reach
Distances sounding through tangles of twisted cords
Talking, talking until our voices fade
Sitting undressed, unkempt, our beds unmade.

XVI

TRUTH

You learned the facts of life and spoke the truth.
Now blizzards of words storm out of ministries,
Hysteric warnings, telling us what to do
To end the plague, issuing pale decrees
For literate germs to read while our cells fight
Onslaughts of microbes mandates cannot control.
History will determine was it right
To banish gatherings that fed our souls
And kept us well. We quarantined good sense
And lost our fighting trim. Monarchs ignore
The physics of medicine, our sure defense,
The wisdom rich inside our bodies' lore.
We live on the edge of death at every turn:
You sent Cain out to danger, to grow, to learn.

XVII

FEAR

We study the curriculum of fear:
It bleeds like acid and seeps between us
Sending us to our rooms with little cheer,
Eating away at our social joys and trust
Making wide spaces for governors to rule.
Afraid to gather against their tyrannies
Like rote learners in a despotic school.
Frightened to stray, we feel our instincts freeze
And shut down for safety. Where did you learn to stand
Against the managers who banish love,
Sentencing freedoms, sharpie pens in hand?
What gave you courage, etched on your cells with blood?
Fear rules over us as tyrants learn its craft,
Reading its abstracts while Satan laughs and laughs.

XVIII

LAW

The rule of Adam, deliberate and kind,
Used reason until your reach broke open
Chaos, unraveling justice, no longer blind,
But, heated by mobs, left cities ash and broken,
No laws enforced but ancient prejudice,
Letting revenge of peoples dominate
Blood feuds old as ancient Aeschylus
Watching the Furies enact their evil fates.
Not knowing the hard struggle for order,
Drunk on the pleasures of ungoverned hate
They devolve to terror's rule, the borders
Kept by fanatics who mock the magistrate.
Fear sets us back past the broad uplands of ease
Where you ambled, safe from old brutalities.

XIX

FORM

Now you must teach us lessons in how to draw,
To make forms beautiful as Adam
From dust, able to show us divinity's law,
Civilizing us; deep in each atom
Frescoes of you in the face of Mary's Son.
Raised at the wheel of clay, holding our joy,
Drawing us out, to see what his hand had done,
Our maker's mercy to build and not destroy.
Like the phoenix we would rise from the ruins here,
Awakened, ready to build again with grace.
Beholding beauty, eternity brought near,
We tremble before the images he traced—
Portents of Paradise carved into stone
Light codes we can divine in our lacy bones.

XX

EARTH

We see intimations in the art
Of life, like marble learning to draw breath,
Pointing to one kneeling down, his heart
Pounding with love, raising wet clay from death,
Breathing into our lungs the air of heaven.
He fills us with invisible drafts of life
To quicken our cells, the flesh that we were given,
Spreading the germ of life so we survive.
Safe in his spirit we labor in flesh to build
New marvels modeled from Eden's prime
Looking toward a city decked with gilt,
Shining like pearl descending out of time.
We kneel with him to raise old Adam's clay
Out of the mud, into a lively play.

XXI

WATER

The glass of water I drank for supper flows
Through my body, then into the ground.
A few weeks later, someone, a friend or foe
In Paris, taking a bath, will splash around
In it, a molecule of liquid cleaned
By nature's filters, earth that gathers it up
Into a drop, soon crashing falls of green
Rushing over the rapids, all from my cup
Swept by the winds into a thunderhead.
It rains down, fresh and crystal clear,
Over Bretagne, into a river bed
Cleansed of infection, its natural taste made pure
Ready for you to bathe in, the glass I drank
Filling your tub like a kidney in the floods of France.

XXII

AIR

The trade winds in the southern hemisphere
Blow microbes from the churning Magellan Straits
Over to Africa, riding the atmosphere
People inhale, unable to isolate
Their bodies from creation. We need plants
Breathing in our carbon breathing out
Air so we survive. Our old great aunts
Rushed to the windows, "Open them," they'd shout,
"Breathe, so your lungs can fill with oxygen,
Blow this dead air out of your stuffy room,
Dilute the fetid quagmire in your den
Dank as the air inside a stony tomb!"
Nothing will grow and not a leaf will last
Without contagion gusting in a stormy blast.

XXIII

BREAD OF LIFE

To eat the bread of life our bodies chew
Breaking divinity into small cells
Quaffing the wine making our spirits new.
We swallow the infection in which we dwell,
It grows in us, feeding on our sin.
We feel it throbbing in our flesh, a force
Like plump seeds sprouting in us as we begin
Breaking the manacles of nature's course
Out of the microbes floating on the air.
We'll catch new complications as they grow
Wandering off to sample worldly fare
Braving contagion from every human woe,
Lowering our masks so we can take and eat
Miracles that kill the deaths we'll meet.

XXIV

ANOTHER GARDEN

Hidden behind the leaves in your suit of green,
An intimation of a garden far away,
Treachery roiling over the vegetable scene.
A kiss, weapons glinting, and wrenched away
We're left solitary, bereft and dark.
He torches great honor, only a silver clink
In the traitor's purse, death in a lovely park.
Eden the stage again where Satan blinks.
Curbing his works and ways you need sound law.
Knowing the gravity of heavy rules
Weighty against sin and its fatal flaws
Betrayers flee the force of their fathers' schools.
Chaos flares up over the unstrung world
No one escapes its wrath, writhing in its whirl.

XXV

LOVE

The traitor kissed the Lord of love, his friend,
Hatred rushing away beneath his feet
Falling into an abyss, a bloody end,
Hell yawning open, the consequences meet
As your son felt him at his heels and turned
In love, his duty to scotch the twice doomed snake
Working the father's will. The coins burned
In his pockets, he wanted justice, nothing could slake
His thirst for vengeance, all of his credit spent.
He fled mercies poured down from the heart of love
To rescue him for the courts of innocence,
Redemption's coinage in the Savior's blood,
The garden ransomed again to Paradise
Love greening the temples of his lies.

XXVI

REMEDY

The remedy is love but not our own.
The sheer abysses of the soul are filled
Only with what pulses from the dawn;
The voice thundered and incarnate will
Finished the drama. Only if we trust
His force borning in us to make us good
Can flesh be healed. He sanctified our dust
With faith, faith in his power, a bloody rood,
Eternity made flesh, another realm
Ready to mold our symptoms to its grace.
Healing our hurt with Gileads of balm.
Horrors of pain and love writhe in his face
Glories of God come down to us
Spanning our fatal separation from his cross.

XXVII

FAREWELL

The autocrats of airy nothingness
Stand on their premises, legislate
Against the laws of nature, their words profess
Dreams without gravity, freedom's loud debate,
With constitutions written from wells of blood.
These barons of good intentions whose naïve rule
Turns bloody, thinking sweet words on paper good.
The gross ideal in which they all were schooled
Shakes down the edifice of these thousand years
Shattering to shards the marble busts of minds
Who wrote Magna Cartas against our fears
Now tattered to shreds making them blind.
I bid them all a last, resigned adieu
Seeing beyond their rubble, a sparkling view.

XXVIII

THE TURN

Because your Son died upon the cross
To bring us heaven, we could live on earth
Fashioning gardens, cathedrals, places for us
To gather, letting our hearts and minds give birth
To shape and beauty pointing to the skies,
You fashioned out of darkness homes and towns
Schooling us in the bare necessities
So we could flourish, mortality drifting down
To foster beauty. I turn my thoughts above
To ecstasies of morning where peace will reign.
Sorrow forgotten, raptures of pure love
Dazzled with light. My bones swollen with pain
Ready to cross the river. Where I am gone
Like lovely evenings on a summer lawn.

XXIX

ETERNITY

Eternity is not a lot of time
But life, the germ in us, that he will raise
Into a weight of glory flesh cannot climb,
Where all will spend an imperishable day
Reveling in the waters from the stream
Flowing beside us, drinking our fill of light.
We will be known and know, like in our dreams
Where every ecstasy lives in sight.
Something all mortal flesh cannot divine
But glimpse in a mirror darkly what now is here:
Inebriations of paradise, its wine
Filling our raised up bodies with abiding cheer.
No darkness there, no tempter to destroy,
This kingdom shimmers with rivers of crystal joy.

XXX

MYSTERY

Tongue cannot tell, nor any word express
The glory we will see when we are changed,
Imperishable, raised from a seed of flesh,
Up and out of Adam's dead remains.
The light will kneel down, breathe into us something new.
The resurrected bodies we'll recognize
As truth sculptures speech to see us through.
Mysteries we will fathom, with new, washed eyes
Beholding the forms of those gone on before
Like answers rushing to greet us, now raised up.
Our hurts healed over, their scars will be no more.
Drink to the lees from heaven's brimming cup—
Not tears, but laughter, dimensions never seen
Dance in the worlds around us, fresh and green.

XXXI

CURIOSITIES

Peering into the mists back to Eden
I see you cultivate the gallant walks
Against the chaos your grasping will had seeded.
Hand in hand, you left sweet Paradise locked.
Now I am turned, viewing you over the rim
Of morning, your progeny toasting your faith,
Death's nemesis, the light surrounding him
With Mary singing. The way to you is death.
Crossing the river, drowning, losing my will
Fearing the lawless one roaring behind,
Flesh struggling, gasping, feeling its marble chill
Creep up my limbs, into a darkened mind—
Shine, lovely Eve, point me to your Son,
Your curiosities feeding the worlds he won.

XXXII

FIRE

O Love of God that cleanses with its fire
And turns the dross to wisps of smoke and ash,
Burn out the corpuscles of earth's desire
And fit my flesh for heaven. In a flash
Transform me into the mystery that words
Can barely utter, but I have long believed.
Fashion my will with the voice I heard
Calling from gardens, green with primeval leaves,
To move forward toward a light that flames
At the center, urging me to pass through
Into a world whose contours I cannot name,
That knows me, the prodigies of life in you.
Consume my faults, O Fire, and raise me up
Into the shining substance of you, my love,

XXXIII

COURAGE

Courage, now as the darkest waters roll
Over my head, and still the wicked one
Taunts my weak faith, as I walk treading below
Into the depths, losing my breath, the Son
Lost to me, nothing, I feel no solid ground,
The promises like buoys ahead, the last
I reach for, then all is dark. No sound,
Nothing. Chaos behind, temptations past
Ephemeral and distant, churning up
Tumults. They perish with me, mortality
Gasping inside me, the shades of smiling Hope
Pointing beyond me, at Shining Ones, a tree,
My feet hit bottom. I see bright air arise.
Light fills my flesh with heaven, the old world dies.

THE GATE OF HEAVEN
AND OTHER POEMS

THE GATE OF HEAVEN

To spend a Sunday afternoon in June
Knowing its transience is what Sabbath is.
Summer is in its pink, the peonies
Nodding with fragrance beneath the summer sun,
The air, blue as the North Atlantic, shines
Over the iris, plumping the lilac trees
Buzzing with visitations of bumblebees.
The sun flagrant with its golden coin.
The beauty that we know that we are given
Fades from our view each day like death.
Today it is enough to hold the light,
Banking its bounty against the night
As nature almost forgets to take a breath,
Surfeits of gold at the very gate of heaven.

EPITHALAMION

(For Bryn and Melinda June 3, 2006)

Sing with me, violets and roses, sing;
Lend music to my speech, sweet peonies,
And all the potentates of air, let ring
The cockle shells of June with melodies
That echo heaven chorusing the glad strains
Of its nuptial refrain.
Bright angels, sing the glories of this day
When young, fresh budding tiny ears of grain
Are greening in the fields where sweet airs play
Their summer psalmody.
Come, let us hymn the grateful thanks we feel
To see them sanctify their promises
Before their formal friends and families
And then into the sable evening steal
As all the planets wheel
Above them making music in the spheres
That only lovers hear,
Celestial harmonies above all light;
Sing softly, galaxies, sweet music through the night.

Now in the blossom of their youth we see
Him by the altar anxiously await
Her entrance as he husbands what is to be.
His heart, all springtime, knows its new estate;
Wedded to life, he watches as she comes
Filled with June's early blooms.
All of nature waits, holding its breath
Stopping to see if life again resumes.
Here in their flesh we see pure hope and faith
Joining for life on earth.
Fruit of their bodies some day will arise
To take their places in a long, studied line
Written in blood and water, sealed and signed;
We see them flowering with joy, their eyes
Beaming with love and sighs.
Now in the early flush of June we hail

The love he will unveil,
Bowing to bless them in the summer light,
Sing softly, galaxies, sweet music through the night.

We see them in their bodies plight their troth
And promise more than flesh alone can keep.
Come, heaven, descend with graces for them both,
Preserve them in their growing so they reap
Harvests as golden as their golden rings,
Ripening as roses sing,
Endless because their love is stronger than death
Fostered by one who died to give their bodies faith.

MOVING IN

The garden, strewn with pink and white
Was planted by another hand,
Another set the angles right
And joined the levels where we stand.
The grace to which we now are heir
Will shape the spirits that we bear.

The children padding on the floors
Delighting in the light that sifts
And dances through the windowed door
Enrich the legacy of gifts
Which echo murmuring older sounds
All dancing as the world turns round.

All these are gifts that we've been given:
To tend the child who dances here
Whose pirouette, a glimpse of heaven,
Has brought divinity so near
We tremble as we catch our breath
And wonder as our hopes take flesh.

EPIGRAMS

PROLOGUE

The sun flames out
at the end of the day.
Everything finally
burns away.

SOCIAL SECURITY

I bend down to help you dress,
tied in knots by an old shoelace.
I'm in my prime, but not so steady
pressing against your fragrant body.
Lean over, I tell you, raising you up
to keep me when I'm old and stooped.

BAPTISM

The river runs deep,
the river runs true,
I say it will be
the death of you.

The flood will come
and do you in
and you will be
what you have not been.

Dead to the world
and the evil one,
raised up new
in flesh and bone.

WILD OATS

Sowing their dreams like wild oats
they do not think will sprout,
they tend no gardens of their own:
wildness takes root.

The offspring of their dreams grow up
and leap to carry on
labors the seeded branches died of
scorched by the burning sun.

Their rows of vines are husbanded
for precious little yield:
the tares beyond the fence grow up
vigorous and wild.

WORTHLESS, HEARTFELT ADVICE

Your voice cracks in the humid church
heavy with used up air:
You sweat into your brand-new clothes,
the world, the flesh are here.

You are the issue of our flesh,
we made you of desire,
the living breathing evidence
of primal need in flower.

The world will have you soon enough:
its wide commercial streets
beckon to every girl and boy,
you don't have long to wait.

So make your promises, my dear,
against the evil foe
wearing an innocent wool suit
beside you, in the know.

A BODY KNOWS

Eternity is the last
of my concerns,
she says, amused at what
a body learns.

NURSERY RHYME

Up above the clouds so high
a plane is flying in the sky.

It thunders like a summer storm
but looks no bigger than a worm

threading its way through bolts of silk,
blue as the ocean, white as milk.

GENETIC CODE

Flesh of my flesh
bone of my bone,
the will you have
is all your own.

THE EXCHANGE

Drifting like gold, this afternoon
dies like a song of Tennyson.

"Sunset," he said, "and evening star…"
things should be different from what they are.

"Bless me," Blake warbled, "little lamb,
save me, save me from what I am."

Roethke cried, "I've been a rake,
spare me, oh, God, for Jesus' sake!"

Jesus sang to his bartered wife,
"I am the way, the truth, the life."

NEGATIVE RESEARCH

History will break your heart. Deep in the stacks
Ferreting through the calendars of time
The supplicant unmasks his hero's mime.
The myth cracks under the certainty of facts,
Shocking enough to sully his pious act.
His noble pose hiding a petty crime,
Our idol crumbles like a statue made of lime,
Who long ago broke his most sacred pacts.

Ah, ha! We cry, he's merely flesh and bone!
We've caught him, laid him bare with our sterile tool,
His secret bleeds from the page, we watch it pool
But cannot staunch it. See how the livid stone
Bloodies our hands in the archives we research
Here in the heart where reason builds its church.

WINTER ROSE

(for Florence on her 100th birthday)

Since centuries are seldom what we bear
Look round the flower that gathers now to see
The sturdy root from which its petals flare,
A rose, a winter rose, still blooming as a tree
Flowering in cold December's fields of light.
These branches she can trace and diagram—
She knows each one, grown dear to her by night
When she remembers them, like cherished lambs,
Her gracious reading of their curious line.
Their history has lived in her these years
Which she has learned carefully to divine,
Her laughter flowering over briars of tears.
And still she blossoms in these winter snows
A flower of light, a pure December rose

WINTER FUNERAL, NORWAY

The mist holds its breath against the light
Shining through the fog over the evergreens;
Black branches etched against the white
Frame the official sorrows of the scene:
The pastor walking in his long black cape
Leading the white casket through the snowy fields
Past rows of gravestones flaked with ashen caps
Followed by mourners suited up like shades.
A study in black and white, except the red
Roses, sprays of them, their petals fall
Glowing like blood upon the white coffin lid,
Their passion incarnadines the mourning pall
Eden goes down in the dust the pastor throws,
Fresh dirt, clattering onto the lawn of snows.

CHRISTMAS CAROL

(for Alice Parker)

Heav'n has no time, but music
Carols all through the night.
We hear the sky above us
Sounding with songs of light.

A word, the first, was spoken,
Breathed on the waters face
Dreaming inchoate darkness
Into all time and space.

Now see inside a manger
One who has left the heav'ns
Pulsing with light that echoes
One word that never ends.

Come to the place, behold it,
Here in an infant's flesh
The word that still is moving
Here in a baby's breath.

THIS LITTLE SONG

This little song
 Cannot be long'
A beam of light
That ends the night
Cannot remain
Nor come again.

I hold it near,
It disappears,
But will not die,
I wonder why?
This little song
Cannot be long.

THE COUNTRY WHERE WE BELONG

(meditations on St. Augustine's *On Christian Doctrine*)

I

VISION

> *...they should ask God to give them vision.*
> *Although I can lift my finger to point something out,*
> *I cannot supply the vision."*
> *Augustine, De doctrina christiana. Prologue*

The heavenly bodies gleam in the velvet dark,
Whether or not I see their prospects shine;
The distant sparkle of the farthest star,
The steep sheer vaults of space in their incline
Speed toward the edges of the universe,
Hurtling beyond, where intellect cannot
Fathom the lines, or with plain words rehearse
The vast midnight of their cosmic plots.
No spectacle can open up the space
Reeling above me or the deeps within
And clear the lenses where these bodies spin—
Open my eyes, where is your lovely face?
For I am blind without the vision you give—
Uncloud the cataracts in which I live.

II

THE WAY

> *...although he is our native country,*
> *He made Himself also the Way to that country.*
> *Augustine's de doctrina christiania. Book I,*

O brighter than all light, my truth, my way,
The country I desire, my native land;
The road I walk is brighter than the day
And pleasant, yet frail nature still demands
I linger in the shadows, take my rest,
Forget the kingdom shining up ahead,
That gleaming city made for all the blest,
The end of all the living and the dead.
Pure light, who came to be our way to light,
Show us the regions where we yearn to dwell,
The means to find the blessed end of night.
Wash from our eyes the stain of sin and hell—
Bathe us in light and make our bodies long
For you, our way, the country where we belong.

III

THE FEAR OF GOD

> *…now this fear will of necessity excite in us the thought*
> *of our mortality and of the death that is before us.*
> Augustine's de doctrina christiana Book II

Pride, the deadliest of all the sins,
Falls by the way when I am filled with fear.
Grabbing my cane to wield against the din
Swarming below, I see shades appear
Creaking and rustling up the bloody stairs.
They know another world beyond my ken,
Beyond the testament of my affairs,
A world of spirits taunting the world of men.
My weapon, meant to bang at a hairy bone,
Flails in the air against them, nothing works—
Locks or alarms or fences of granite stone.
Here in the mind darkness takes shape and lurks.
Nothing but prayer can keep such terror out,
Prayer that unseats the wisdom of my doubt.

IV

HOLY SCRIPTURE

*A man fearing God diligently seeks his will
in the Holy Scriptures.
Augustine, de doctrina christiana, Book III,*

(For Jeanette Naley on her 90th birthday)

When in the pale of sorrow she reached for light
To guide her through shadows she did not expect,
She dipped into treasures she had learned to recite
Gravely while still a girl. Now they reflect
Their beauty in her mettle and hold her up,
Words our thesaurus knows a woman needs
To stand against a grief, to drain its cup
And make of the galling chalice a sanguine creed.
Here in the Book she found a will to match
Her own, to which her dignity would bow
And in the gesture she was given strength,
A rectitude that nothing could dispatch,
Shining as much as formal flesh allows,
Made to endure with grace for any length.

V

HOPE

*...for the knowledge of a good hope makes a man
not boastful, but sorrowful.*
Augustine, de doctrina christiana Book II,

Hope, like great music, draws us toward God's love,
Filling our hearts with sorrow for what we know
Is absent, the motion of the air above
Aches in our melancholic humors, and flows
From the clear song of his celestial spring.
Like cut crystal, it sparkles when music speaks—
Sound refracting light, colors that sing
And make us long for heaven, as beauty breaks
Over our heads, like Sunday morning bells
Calling our sympathetic flesh to come
Toward the bright place ahead. Even our cells
Long for their end, dying to be home
To bow like blossoms before the river's light
Drinking in airs as they play upon our sight.

VI

TURNING TOWARD THINGS ETERNAL

..and turning away from these, fixes his attention on things eternal.
Augustine de doctrina christiana II

Dawn burns off the shimmering clouds of mist
When we can see what lasts, what will endure,
Places that draw us toward them though we resist
Until a firm purpose draws us there
Out where the light is shining, blinding white,
When transitory things have melted away—
The house, the farm, the city's twinkling lights,
Where darkest night and morning dance and play.
Though we can see you in the lovely things
That perish, give us strength so we can find
The source, the trilling brook of light that springs
Above, the point that orients the mind
Guiding our skiffs up through imagined skies
To you, our Morning Star and Paradise.

VII

COUNSEL OF COMPASSION

> *…in the counsel of compassion, he cleanses his soul,*
> *which is violently agitated, and disturbs him*
> *with base desires.*
> Augustine de doctrina christiana II

Ah! If our hearts could be healed of their base desires
And love the neighbor as we ought or should
Turning away from feverish things, the fires
That burn in our flesh for what we feel is good,
But later regret. To train our strength and wills
To care for those nearest, even our enemies,
And cleanse the hatred that makes sick and kills.
We need a cure to end our maladies,
Some tablets to chew against these mortal woes.
Give me a stronger medicine than I
Keep in my arsenal, a lethal dose
To put to death the sickness that must die:
Love that would feed on pleasure for itself,
Love that grows bitter on its glassy shelf.

VIII

PURITY OF HEART

*A holy man will be so single and so pure in heart
that he will not step aside from the truth.
Augustine de doctrina christiana II*

To be pure, pure in heart, to walk by faith
And not by sight, so that nothing, not even love
Of family, friend or foe, the threat of death
Can turn us from our path to the courts above.
To be single-minded, not to step aside
From what is true, to have strength, an iron will,
Under the gaze that flesh cannot abide,
Not to be diverted, to move forward until
The truth, sparkling as Paradise now shines
Before us, then nothing can undo our way.
We will see life blossom—human, divine—
As Love draws us toward itself; we'll sway
Dancing in circles round the point of light
Cleansed of the base desires that blind our sight.

IX

WISDOM

> *...stranger to the world and home in heaven...*
> Augustine *de doctrina christiana* II

Himself the habitation he has built
To house his own, he gives us Paradise
In his own flesh, takes our sin and guilt,
Invests us with his kingdom. We grow wise
Because he is our Lord. We bow in prayer
And know we are but creatures, with the means
He made for us to pleasure in, and share
The gifts he gives us for the times between.
We move toward ends we know as love.
He draws us toward himself, his glorious flesh
Shining and risen in his heaven above
That we can know today, green and fresh.
When he is here our heaven is begun
And we are home, his body is our sun.

X

THE SHAPE OF ELOQUENCE

*They fulfilled them because they were eloquent;
they did not apply them that they might be eloquent.
Augustine de doctrina christiana Book IV*

(for Ann Pederson)

The shape of all our syntax, the eloquence
Our tongues stumble over, fell from her lips
Separating foolish wit from wise sense
With the clear precision of her British clip.
A Kansas girl from the farm she left for verse,
Learning the logic of setting the truth down
In spare sentences of lasting worth,
The music of a phrase moving around.
She taught us rural things, the concrete names
Of Scripture's world, the winnower, the chaff
Floating bright flecks of gold in the blue sky
Evidence of unseen things she claimed:
Judgment, the great division, the shepherd's staff,
The shining substances that passed us by.

XI

ELOQUENT WISDOM

*There are men of the church who treat Scriptures
not only wisely but eloquently..."
Augustine de doctrina christiana IV*

*(for Michael Rogness on his retirement
as Professor of Homiletics at Luther Seminary)*

His droll wit, his easiness with words
Come from his heritage, the pleasant lines
Of natural grace and Scripture where his Lord
Teaches the deeps of meaning in his mines,
His study in the rifts of these bright jewels
Has made him eloquent, but first off wise.
We hear it when he speaks, so natural,
Then tenderly opening a surprise
As light that he has lived with all his life
Shines in his being when he starts to talk.
His sermons hold the treasure up to the light
Which gleams about his body as he walks
Where eloquence and wisdom are closely bound
As his elegant plain speaking comes around.

XII

THE PLENITUDE OF JOY

*…The plenitude and the end of the Law and of all the sacred Scripture
is the love of a Being which is to be enjoyed
and of a being that can share that enjoyment with us.
Augustine de doctrina christiania Book I, xxxv*

The green world filled with lovely things is ours—
Blossoms bursting out of their swollen buds
In May, the candles flaming in the mirrors
As dusk deepens around us in the woods.
The spacious heaven we love but cannot see
Spreads out its gauzy veil around us
Like spring mist, closer than it appears to be.
While every day harvest looms more close
We know the country that we love is here
And we have stopped along its way to dine,
The blue-veined cheese, the juicy red ripe pear.
To take the silver evenings we've been given,
The conversation, ruddy as the wine,
This plenitude of joy we know as heaven.

Published in *Lutheran Forum,* Summer, 2008

THE ROSE

The rose's beauty stays
But few and lovely days,
The thorns remain behind
With hurts our flesh can find.
Our sorrow always shows
The transience of the rose.

The brambles still remain
And prick us with their pain,
They'll die in floods of light
That bring an end to night
As heaven's beauty flows
Into God's crystal rose.

Gracia Grindal, Luther Seminary Professor of Rhetoric Emerita, received her MFA from the University of Arkansas in Poetry in 1969. She taught Creative Writing at Luther College, Homiletics and Hymnody at Luther Seminary in St. Paul MN. She has written several books of poetry over the past forty years, *Sketches Against the Dark,* (1984) *A Revelry of Harvest,* (2002) *The Sword of Eden* (2018) and *Jesus the Harmony: Gospel Sonnets for 366 Days* (Fortress 2021) favoring the sonnet form. This latest book, a continuation of poetry about our Mother Eve, continues in that tradition with other formal poetry written over the past decade.

www.ingramcontent.com/pod-product-compliance
Lightning Source LLC
Chambersburg PA
CBHW020340170426
43200CB00006B/445